Special Brothers and Sisters

other Jessica Kingsley Publishers books for children

Different Like Me
My Book of Autism Heroes
Jennifer Elder
Illustrations by Marc Thomas and Jennifer Elder
ISBN 1 84310 815 1 hb

Wishing On the Midnight Star
My Asperger Brother
Nancy Ogaz
ISBN 1 84310 757 0

Stephen Harris in Trouble
A Dyspraxic Drama in Several Clumsy Acts
Tim Nichol
ISBN 1 84310 134 3

Adam's Alternative Sports Day
An Asperger Story
Jude Welton
ISBN 1 84310 300 1

of related interest for adults

Brothers and Sisters of Disabled Children
Peter Burke
ISBN 1 84310 043 6

The Views and Experiences of Disabled Children and Their Siblings
A Positive Outlook
Clare Connors and Kirsten Stalker
ISBN 1 84310 127 0

Special Children, Challenged Parents
The Struggles and Rewards of Raising a Child with a Disability
Robert A. Naseef
ISBN 1 84310 047 9

Growing Up with Disability
Edited by Carol Robinson and Kirsten Stalker
ISBN 1 85302 568 2
Research Highlights in Social Work 34

Special Brothers and Sisters

Stories and Tips for Siblings of Children with a Disability or Serious Illness

Edited by Annette Hames and Monica McCaffrey

Illustrated by Brendan McCaffrey

Jessica Kingsley Publishers
London and Philadelphia

First published in 2005
by Jessica Kingsley Publishers
116 Pentonville Road
London N1 9JB, UK
and
400 Market Street, Suite 400
Philadelphia, PA 19106, USA

www.jkp.com

Library of Congress Cataloging in Publication Data

Special brothers and sisters : stories and tips for siblings of children with a disability or serious illness / edited by Annette Hames and Monica McCaffrey ; illustrated by Brendan McCaffrey.-- 1st American pbk. ed.

p. cm.

Includes index.

ISBN-13: 978-1-84310-383-7 (pbk. : alk. paper)

ISBN-10: 1-84310-383-4 (pbk. : alk. paper) 1. Children with disabilities--Family relationships. 2. Brothers and sisters of people with disabilities. 3. Children with disabilities--Family relationships--Case studies. I. Hames, Annette, 1957- II. McCaffrey, Monica, 1963- III. McCaffrey, Brendan.

HQ773.6.S64 2005
306.87--dc22

2005015455

British Library Cataloguing in Publication Data

A CIP catalogue record for this book is available from the British Library

ISBN-10: 1 84310 383 4
ISBN-13: 978 1 84310 383 7

Printed and Bound in Great Britain by
Athenaeum Press, Gateshead, Tyne and Wear

To all the children and young people who generously shared their stories with us

Acknowledgements

We wish to thank Sorcha, Róisín, Eleanor, Christopher and Susannah for suggesting ways to make the writing easier for children to understand. Thanks also to Brendan McCaffrey for the great illustrations and cover artwork.

Contents

A note to brothers and sisters

Dear brother or sister,

This book is for you. We want you to know that you are not alone. There are lots of other children and young people who grow up with a brother or sister with special needs, disability or serious illness.

In this book, **siblings** from 40 families talk about growing up with their brother or sister. Next to each story we have written a tip that you may find helpful. You can read this book on your own or with a parent. The Contents page will help you find a sibling who is the same age as you, or is talking about something you are interested in.

At the end of each story, *Keywords explained* explains the words that are written in **bold** letters. *Find out more*, at the back of the book (pages 86–90), is where you can find out more about the different disabilities and illnesses that the siblings talk about in this book. There is also a list of organisations you can contact if you need any more help.

We would love to know what you think about this book. You can email your views to us – our contact details are given at the end of this book (on page 94).

Enjoy reading the book!

Keywords explained

- A **sibling** is just another word for a brother or sister.

A note to parents

Dear parent or carer,

This book is for the siblings of children with special needs, disability or serious illness. It has been written in response to parents saying that there is not enough written information for siblings.

We want your son or daughter to know that he or she is not alone or unusual. We have collected stories from siblings in 40 families. In these families there are children with a wide range of special needs, disabilities and serious illness. The siblings range in age from 3½ to 18 years. We hope that your son or daughter will read or listen to these stories and identify with some of the siblings and their experiences.

You may like to read through these stories with your son or daughter or let him or her read alone. We suggest that you look through the book before giving it to your child. There may be some issues you want to discuss with your child before he or she reads it. Next to each story there is a box giving tips and more information about a topic that has been mentioned. We have written about issues that are common concerns for many siblings, such as jealousy, embarrassment and worry about the future. Some of the tips in the boxes encourage the sibling to talk with you about the issue.

At the end of each story the section called *Keywords explained* explains the words that are in bold. The *Find out more* section, at the back of the book (pages 86–90), gives a brief description, for children, of the disabilities and illnesses that are referred to in the stories.

The stories have been organized by age. If you are looking for a particular illness or condition in a story, the index at the back of the book will help you to find it.

Many parents whose children are featured in this book said that the process of writing the stories was very beneficial for the siblings. We hope that your children find them helpful too. You can email your views to us – our details are provided at the back of this book.

He won't be able to walk and talk

Jessica, 3½, talks about her brother Haydn, 19 weeks, who has a **chromosome disorder**.

Haydn was poorly. He went to a different hospital. He was poorly, in an **incubator**. He won't be able to walk and talk. The chromosome is in his body. The doctor checked his tummy. I've seen a picture of children like Haydn – one had spaces in his teeth. Haydn has to wear his shoes to keep his feet straight. He had plasters on his toes first. He had green eyes when he was born. I kiss him.

Do you know why your brother or sister needs a lot of help?

Ask your parent to help you find out more. Ask if they would:

- tell you more about your brother or sister
- show you a picture of other children who are similar
- take you to meet other children like your brother or sister
- take you to meet other siblings.

Keywords explained

- **Chromosome disorder** – take a look at the *Find out more* section on page 87.
- **Incubator** – a special bed that newborn babies go into in hospital to keep them warm.

I like it best when I'm tickling her

Emmy, 4, talks about her sister Kirsty, 18, who has **cerebral palsy**.

She laughs. I like reading Christmas cards to her. I climb in bed with her. I like tickling her. I like playing beads with her. Pink beads. I make necklaces. I put them on me and Kirsty.

I love Kirsty. I like it best when I'm tickling her.

Do you have fun with your brother or sister?

Here are some fun activities you can try:

- Make hand shadows on the bedroom wall.
- See who can sit longest without laughing.
- Make newspaper snowballs and throw them at each other.
- Draw faces on balloons and then play throw and catch.
- Listen to a story tape together.
- Look at picture books and tell a story to your brother or sister.
- Make up stories.
- Make funny faces together.
- Make funny noises together.
- Play tickling games.
- Sing nursery rhymes.

Keywords explained

- **Cerebral palsy** – take a look at the *Find out more* section on page 87.

Sometimes she pulls my hair

Chanel, 4, talks about her sister Amydane, 7, who has **ADHD**.

I play with her and do nice things with her. We make things. I like going on her bike. She can ride her bike. I ride Amy's bike. Sometimes she says, 'Hey, get off the seesaw'. She just said get off and then she pushed me on the floor and I banged my head off the floor. In the garden. It hurt me.

She's naughty. She's got to have tablets so she can be good and be nice. To help her. She's got new tablets, yellow ones. She just annoys me, then she's naughty, that's why she's got to have her tablets.

I like her. Sometimes she pulls my hair. I don't like it when she pulls someone else's hair.

Sometimes she bangs my baby brother on things. She dropped him on the floor.

Does your brother or sister ever hurt you?

Many siblings live with a brother or sister who has very difficult behaviour. Do you get hit, bitten, have your hair pulled, or get hurt in any other way? If so, here are some things you can do:

- Tell your parent or teacher about it.
- Ask the social worker or health worker or nurse, who visits your brother or sister, to help you with it.
- If you know there are things that make your brother or sister really angry, it is better not to do them.

Keywords explained

- **ADHD** – take a look at the *Find out more* section on page 86.

I go to school with my brother

Carla, 5, talks about her brother Jack, 7, who has **cerebral palsy**.

I go to school with my brother. I play with my brother. Jack plays with me on the computer. We take Jack for walks if he is feeling sad. I read a story to Jack. Jack will choose a toy to play with and I help him. I see Jack in the playground. Me, Rebecca and Chloe push him. Me and Jack saw Mickey Mouse in a show which we watched. My brother watches television with me. He can stand but mummy needs to help him stand. He can roll around. He cannot talk. He cannot walk. Jack is nice.

How do you spend time with your brother or sister?

Siblings often spend a lot of time with their brothers and sisters who have special needs. What things do you do with your brother or sister? Can you think of:

- three things you do together at home
- three things you do together outdoors
- three things you do together in the school holidays?

Keywords explained

- **Cerebral palsy** – take a look at the *Find out more* section on page 87.

I feel a bit left out

Jane, 5, talks about her two brothers who have **MPS disease**.

It's difficult for my brothers. I can do things they can't and it's not fair on them.

When I go to the MPS **conference** and there are lots of children with things wrong, I feel a bit left out and I want to be like my brothers.

One of my friends asked me what **hearing aids** are.

Do you feel left out sometimes?

Other siblings feel like this too. Some of the suggestions below may help:

- If you have friends the same age as you, maybe you can sometimes go and play with them or they can come to your house.
- Ask your parent if they know any other children like you. Maybe your parent can arrange for you to meet other children who have a brother or sister with special needs.
- Your parent won't mind if you tell them that you feel left out; it helps to talk about how you feel.

Keywords explained

- **MPS disease** – take a look at the *Find out more section* on pages 89–90.
- **Conference** – a big meeting of people who are interested in the same thing.
- **Hearing aid** – a tiny plastic gadget that fits inside a person's ear to help them hear.

I felt sad when Ginni was in hospital

Lakshmi, 5, talks about her sister Ginni, 2, who has **leukaemia**.

I gave some of my **bone marrow** to help make Ginni better. I felt sad when Ginni was in hospital. I missed her and also my parents, because they took turns to look after Ginni in hospital.

I miss having baths with my sister. We don't do that now she has a **Hickman line**, which I wish would be taken out – it upsets me very much. Ginni is now at home and getting better.

There are lots of things she can't do, like going to restaurants or playing with other children, but I don't mind. This is only until she gets stronger.

I love mum, dad, and especially Ginni, even though she does fight with me. I am glad we are together.

Do you miss your brother or sister when they go into hospital?

Lots of siblings miss their brother or sister and parent when they have to stay in hospital. Some siblings get upset about the treatment that their brother or sister needs to have. Some of the suggestions below may help:

- Tell your parent you really miss him or her, when he or she needs to stay with your brother or sister.
- Make a special card for your parent.
- Make a special card for your brother or sister.
- Get someone to take you to the hospital often.
- Ask your parent how long your brother or sister will be in hospital and make a calendar to count the days.

- Ask your parent why your brother or sister needs treatment.

Keywords explained

- **Leukaemia** – take a look at the *Find out more* section on page 89.
- **Bone marrow** – spongy stuff inside bones. It produces special blood cells (called white blood cells) that protect people against infection and make sure oxygen (the part of air we breathe) gets to every corner of the body.
- **Hickman line** – a very thin tube that goes into a large vein in the chest. Then medicine can go through the tube into the person's blood.

Craig's really good in goal

Liam, 6, talks about his brother Craig, 12, who has a **chromosome disorder**.

He's got a missing chromosome; he's a little bit different to me. He's got **learning difficulties** and he has to do baby's work like, in the reception class. He can't do my kind of work, like the homework I have to bring home – he wouldn't be able to do that because it's too hard for him. And he doesn't have to do **SATS** but I do have to. My mam has to help him with his homework, give him extra help. Sometimes he puts his thumb in his mouth and he just stares.

Me and Craig play football games on the computer. He's just won for the first time – I always beat him but now he's won once. We play football as well, and Craig's really good in goal.

What things can your brother or sister do well?

Some people may think that your brother or sister cannot do much but you know that he or she can. How many things can you think of, that your brother or sister does well? Think of:

- things to do with games or sport
- things to do with food
- things to do with moving
- things to do with school
- things to do with their voice
- things to do with being caring or loving
- things to do with making other people happy.

Keywords explained

- **Chromosome disorder** – take a look at the *Find out more* section on page 87.
- **Learning disabilities/Learning difficulties** – take a look at the *Find out more* section on page 89.
- **SATS** – special work at school called Standard Assessment Tests.

Sometimes I get quite embarrassed

Nicole, 6, talks about her brother Liam, 8, who has **autism**.

He doesn't talk. When he's in the house and I get my hair done, he doesn't like it. I don't know if he's jealous or he's worried it's hurting me. He doesn't like me screaming and crying. He gets upset when I'm upset.

He screams and cries all the time. He doesn't like the noise. Sometimes he gets angry at balls and at other things. Sometimes he doesn't.

He's okay. I like giving him things to eat. He eats oranges, bananas and raisins and sausages. Sometimes when he's angry, I give him things to play with and that gets him happier. Like his bouncy ball. I sometimes blow bubbles and sometimes he gets angry and sometimes he doesn't. He picks flowers and snaps them in half, so we don't usually get flowers. He eats soil, but we've covered it over with new grass.

Sometimes I get quite embarrassed when my friends come to our house and Liam poos his nappy. They don't know why he has to wear nappies and they think at his age he should go to the toilet.

Sometimes I get quite sad too. I would love Liam to play with me, but he never does. He just wants to twiddle things and spin around and around on his own.

I wish Liam could talk so when he screams and cries he could tell mammy what is wrong and she could make him feel better.

Do you feel embarrassed when your friends come round?

Sometimes siblings worry about asking new friends to their house. They wonder what the friends will do when they meet the person with special needs for the first time. Here are some things that can help:

- Tell your friends about your brother or sister before they visit.
- Explain that your brother or sister has a disability or illness. Tell them how this makes his or her behaviour, speech, movement or health different from other children.
- Talk to friends about some of the good things as well as the difficult things.

Keywords explained

- **Autism** – take a look at the *Find out more* section on page 86.

He wakes me up

Jack, 7, talks about his brother Ethan, 5, who has **autism**.

I'm 7 and Ethan's 5. The thing that's different about Ethan is that he always watches the same programme on the TV – *Blue's Clues*, and the same bit.

There are some things we can't do because of Ethan. I asked my mam if we could go to see *Harry Potter* and she said only if we're alone. Ethan couldn't go because he'd make a lot of noise. It's a bit annoying. I get a bit of peace when I go to friends' houses. It's nice to go to someone else's house for peace. I can go in the garden. Ethan always wants me to come back in. He pulls me in.

If someone could take him out I'd probably be happy. I could play on my Game Boy. It's hard when he's here, he makes so much noise, it's hard to concentrate. If he went out I'd probably have a rest.

I never tell my friends about him. They've met him. They've not asked any questions. I don't like them asking questions.

Also, he nearly always stays up all night. He wakes me up. He doesn't play with me much. He likes watching TV, so I play on my own. Mostly I play on the computer. He's always been like this. I get on with him a bit. I don't do anything with him.

Do you get woken up at night by your brother or sister?

Some brothers and sisters with special needs are very noisy at night. This can mean that a sibling gets woken up a lot and feels tired in the daytime. Being tired makes it hard to do work at school and can make you feel grumpy and fed up. You need sleep to be healthy and to be able to learn easily. The suggestions below may help:

- Talk to your parent about being disturbed at night.
- Ask your parent to tell your teacher that you get woken up at night.
- Maybe sometimes you can have a sleepover with a friend or a relative so you get a good night's sleep.

Keywords explained

- **Autism** – take a look at the *Find out more* section on page 86.

I am thinking he might die

Laurie, 7½, talks about his brother Archie, 9, who has **cystic fibrosis** *and his sister Katy, 5, who is* **deaf**.

I like getting on with Archie – he is good fun. We play Lego, and we both do guitar lessons. Sometimes we play on the PlayStation.

I know that cystic fibrosis makes your **sputum** quite thick and it bungs up your lungs a bit. Sometimes he has to go to hospital and have check-ups. Usually I go with him. When he is in for quite a long time, I can only go for visits. Sometimes he has to go in to have his Gripper needle put in. That is a needle that goes in a patch in his body, with metal in it. Once he was in for a month or two months. I do not really know why he has to go in.

Sometimes I worry about him. I just worry. I am thinking, he might be so poorly, he might die. I am just worried; I know he would not die. He does not really talk about it, and I do not tell him I am worried.

Katy's quite nice, but when she has got no **hearing aids** in she gets quite stroppy because she cannot hear us. We have to shout. It is quite loud. I do not worry about her very much because she does not have to go in to hospital.

Do you worry if your brother or sister gets ill?

Siblings who have a brother or sister who is very ill worry about them at times. They may be afraid that they might catch the illness too, like catching a cold. Or they may be afraid that their brother or sister might die. If you think like this, here are some things that may help:

- Ask your parent to explain the illness, so you can understand how your brother or sister got it.
- Tell your parent about your worries and fears. Even though they may be worried too, it is OK to ask them questions about the illness and the treatments. They can tell you what is happening with your brother or sister, and how serious the problem really is.
- See if your parent can arrange for a doctor or nurse to explain things to you.

Keywords explained

- **Cystic fibrosis** – take a look at the *Find out more* section on page 87.
- **Deaf** – take a look at the *Find out more* section on page 87.
- **Sputum** – very thick spit.
- **Hearing aid** – a tiny plastic gadget that fits inside a person's ear to help them hear.

I feel sad because she isn't in my school

William, 7¾, talks about his sister Sophie, 6½, who has **Sanfilippo disease**.

Sophie always stands in front of the television. She sings Old MacDonald, Ring-a-ring of roses, Wheels on the bus, 1, 2, 3, 4, 5, and her favourite is Row, row, row your boat.

She screams very loudly and throws things about. She also chews Leo's nose (my toy lion) and her toy bone! She chews puzzles and books as well. She smacks daddy and mummy on the back. She always chews her cups so she can't get any juice out of them. She poos loads and runs around. She has a special chair to eat in to stop her from escaping. We have to put special powder in her juice and fruit because it helps her.

I like to push Sophie in her wheelchair and mummy or dad will stop me rushing down the hill with her. She put her foot down the toilet and got her foot and sock and trousers wet! Sophie threw her duck bread in the lake when the bag was tied with a knot. Poor ducks!

When we were littler, when we were in the bath, Sophie turned on the hot tap, then I slipped on the bath floor!

I feel sad because she isn't in my school and because she has to go to a hospital – Great Ormond Street – and a **hospice** called Keech.

Do you feel sad sometimes?

Sometimes siblings feel sad because their brother or sister is very ill. Or they may feel sad when they think about the things their brother or sister cannot do. If you feel sad, some of the suggestions below may help:

- Have a cry; many people feel a bit better after a cry.
- Write about your sadness in a notebook.
- Draw a picture about your sadness.
- Ask a parent for a hug or a chat.
- Tell your parent that you feel sad.

Keywords explained

- **Sanfilippo disease** – take a look at **MPS disease** in the *Find out more* section on pages 89–90.
- **Hospice** – a place where very ill children can stay with their families and be cared for by doctors and nurses.

Me and my sister tease him

Daniel, 8, talks about his brother Jamie, 10, who has **Down syndrome**. *(He also has a sister, Stacey, 14, who has Down syndrome. Both Jamie and Stacey are adopted.)*

Jamie is silly. When we talk to him, he keeps on saying, 'What does that mean?' Because he doesn't understand. He doesn't understand when I'm reading him a story book. I say, 'What's this word?' and he says a different word than it is. He can read good, but a few words he gets stuck on. It's hard for him. He goes to a special school.

He gets into fights with me. I don't like it when he shouts and gets into a mood, when he doesn't get his own way. When he asks mum in the morning, 'Can I have a Screwball, an ice-cream?' and when she says no, he goes upstairs and gets in a tantrum. He makes a noise on the floor with his feet. It's just that.

He likes to practise playing on the PlayStation. He goes on with me. He plays with me on football games. I like showing him. I like playing games with him. I like playing with toys. Me and my sister tease him and then he goes mad and bangs his head against the wall.

Do you ever tease or annoy your brother or sister?

Many siblings tease their brother or sister. This may seem like fun at times, but usually ends up making a brother or sister have a tantrum or throw things around. You can also get hurt if he or she gets very angry. It is better to encourage your brother or sister to behave in a good way. Whenever he or she behaves well:

- say 'Well done'
- give him or her a hug
- give him or her a toy or something nice
- smile at him or her
- clap your hands.

Keywords explained

- **Down syndrome** – take a look at the *Find out more* section on page 87.

I like to see people talking to my brother

Elizabeth, 8, talks about her brother James, 5, who has severe **learning and physical disabilities**.

My brother James is nice to play with – he laughs when I clap my hands and sing happy birthday to him. He likes to play with baby card books, watching the washing machine on spin, he loves Bear in the Big Blue House videos. I do not mind that he has it on a lot, I just play with my dolls. I love to hug and tickle my brother, it makes me laugh. I get scared when he has a **fit** and has to go to hospital.

When we go out James shouts, does raspberries and his very own duck noise. Some people stare and some people say what lovely curly hair he has got. I am not too keen on the people who stare because that's rude and a bit mean. I like to see people talking to my brother; he cannot talk but they make him laugh.

I love my brother very much.

How do you like people to be with your brother or sister?

Some people are not sure what to do when they meet someone with a disability for the first time. What do you like people to do, when they meet your brother or sister? If other children ask you what to do, here are some things you might say:

- 'Talk to them.'
- 'Smile at them.'
- 'Be friendly and kind to them.'
- 'Let them join in with games.'
- 'Treat them like other children.'

Keywords explained

- **Learning disabilities/Learning difficulties** – take a look at the *Find out more* section on page 89.
- **Physical disabilities** – take a look at the *Find out more* section on page 90.
- **Fit** – take a look at **Epilepsy** in the *Find out more* section on page 88.

We watch TV and he gets all excited

Lewis, 8, talks about his brother Sunny, 5, who has **cerebral palsy**.

Every Christmas I used to wish, I want my baby brother better. Now I just love him the way he is and I just want him to stay the way he is. He's perfect. If I want him to be quiet, he's quiet all the time. When he's asleep I cuddle him in the face and he goes all red. We have a bath together, dad tells him stories and he laughs.

I like him the way he is, better or not better, I still love him. If he was okay, I wouldn't know how to speak to him, what language to use. He's great the way he is.

If I tell him a joke, even if it doesn't make sense, he still laughs.

When I look after him, he can't speak because he's disabled, but when I say something, even if it doesn't make sense, he still laughs.

I make a bed on the floor with two big pillows and a quilt and we lie on the sheet and cuddle each other and watch TV, like the Tweenies, and he gets all excited. I've helped to undress him and dress him when he's going out. I sprayed talcum powder all over him so he was all white. Like a ghost. I put hair gel on him, but if it's in big lumps I can't get it out. Sometimes that can be a bit difficult, when his hair's all stuck and spiky.

If your brother sticks his hands out and cuddles you then he's trying to say that he loves you. Some children might do something else. Sometimes they blow kisses; that means they love you.

If you've got a son or daughter who is disabled, and they know how to count, you could say count five kisses for me and they'll blow five kisses and you know they can count. It's a different kind of way to using your fingers.

What activities have you tried with your brother or sister?

Some children who are disabled can only do things for a very short time. Just try a new activity for a short time to see how it goes. You may need adult help to do some of these activities. You could try doing activities together, such as:

- blowing bubbles
- rolling a ball back and forth on the floor
- playing with hand puppets
- taking turns to hide toys around the house
- indoor skittles
- playing doctors
- tag
- frisbee
- shopping for clothes
- listening to music
- card games
- hairstyling and make-up
- acting out a story while someone else reads it
- clapping songs
- computer games
- watching films.

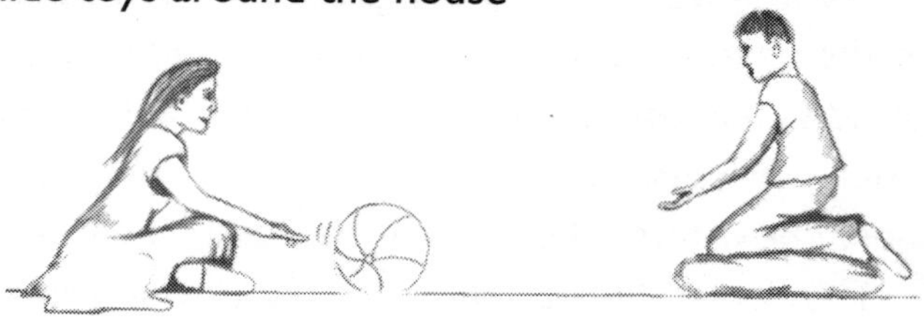

Keywords explained

- **Cerebral palsy** – take a look at the *Find out more* section on page 87.

You know how to do more stuff

Tamara, 8, talks about her brothers Toby, 6, who has **arthrogryposis** *and Davy, 11, who has* **cerebral palsy** *and is* **deaf**.

I have two disabled brothers and a baby one that's not disabled. At first I was worried that my youngest brother Hugo would be disabled too. But that didn't happen for two reasons – because my brothers' disabilities don't run in the family and because my disabled brothers were adopted.

I think I'll tell you about my little brother Toby first. He's a nice sort of chap. He's quite clever for his age. He is always smiling and laughing although sometimes that gets to his head and he is silly, but only like any other 6-year-old who is excited.

Sometimes I can't do things because of my brothers, like when we went to the Lake District and I wanted to climb a mountain but my brothers couldn't manage it. That makes me a little bit sad. Sometimes I don't like it when everyone's looking at him and I want them to pay some attention to me. I know he's different but he's still just a person like me.

Toby is really easy to write about but Davy is extremely difficult to describe. Davy's problems are more out of hand because you can't control the way he thinks. I don't like it when he grabs me around the neck trying to cuddle me, because it hurts a lot because he's really strong. As he is deaf I have learnt to do **sign language** and I get the opportunities to practise my signing at bedtime when he has taken his **hearing aids** off, and in the morning before he puts them on. When people see me doing this they think I'm really clever because they don't know how to sign but they wish they could. I would like to help my friends learn how to sign.

Toby and Davy are both disabled but that is the only thing that's the same about them. Apart from that they are completely different.

There are good things and bad things about having disabled brothers. The bad thing is that sometimes you can't do the things you want and they might be annoying and you don't always get the attention. But the good things are you know how to do more stuff and make friends more easily and you can stand out sometimes. I'm glad my brothers are like they are, otherwise they wouldn't be them and my life would be different.

What are the good things about being a sibling?

There are lots of good things that siblings get from having a brother or sister with a disability or special needs. What are the good things for you? See if you can write a long list and add something new every day for a week. These are some of the things other siblings find good:

- Getting to the front of the queue in theme parks.
- Going to a sibling group.
- Meeting a famous person.
- Being able to park near the shops.
- Playing with their brothers' and sisters' toys.

Keywords explained

- **Arthrogryposis** – take a look at the *Find out more* section on page 86.
- **Cerebral palsy** – take a look at the *Find out more* section on page 87.
- **Deaf** – take a look at the *Find out more* section on page 87.
- **Sign language** – using your hands to talk to someone.
- **Hearing aid** – a tiny plastic gadget that fits inside a person's ear to help them hear.

People stare

Anna, 9, talks about her brother Paul, 5, who has **global developmental delay**.

He stands out when he's playing with others – he looks different. He looks like he's galloping. He looks disabled, though not usually to other people.

He's settled well at school. He's not as good at writing as the others; he has to use special pencils. It would be easier if he was at a different school. In some ways that would be good. But in another school he wouldn't see his friends: he's made really good friends at this school.

The bad thing is that people know he's disabled in my school. If his trouser is up and his leg **splint** is showing, I pull his trouser down. It's more bad for me when he's at my school because I don't want people to know and ask questions. I don't say he's disabled, I say he's hurt his leg.

I don't mind going swimming with him; he doesn't have splints, and he looks so cute. I don't like it in the summer, he wears shorts, and everyone can see his splints. People stare. They say, 'Is that your brother? What's on his leg?' I say he's hurt his leg and he has to wear it.

Do people stare at your brother or sister when you're out?

It can feel really embarrassing when this happens. People stare when they see something or someone different. People are usually just curious but some people can be rude; this can happen when a disabled person goes into a café or shop. Sometimes siblings worry a lot about this and notice it every time they go out. If this happens to you, the suggestions below may help:

- Ask your parent if you can stay at home or with a friend sometimes.
- When you go out, think of all the nice things that are happening – like the people who look friendly, the things you like in the shops, the nice food you are eating. When we concentrate really hard on the nice things, we don't notice the other things so much.
- Tell your parent that people are staring.

Keywords explained

- **Global developmental delay** – take a look at the *Find out more* section on page 88.
- **Splint** – something firm that supports an arm or leg, if the wrist or ankle is not strong enough.

We have to play things with Faris instead

Ayla, 9, and Amani, 6, talk about their brother Faris, 3, who is disabled.

Faris was born **prematurely** and was really tiny – he weighed 1lb 5oz. He has got a **tracheostomy** to let him breathe by himself because his air pipe isn't big enough. He's had it all his life. Because he's got that in, he can't really eat solids so he has a **gastrostomy** in his stomach as well, so that he can be fed from a bag. When he was first born he was in hospital for over a year, and after that he was in and out lots of times. He hasn't been in for ages now though. When he's in hospital we worry but we can go and see him.

Faris can't talk, but he can do a bit of **sign language** and he makes noises. He can't express his feelings though, and that's why sometimes he hits people. We understand that more now, but other people – like our cousins – don't always understand that if he hits them, sometimes it's his way of saying 'Come and play', because he can't express himself.

Faris is very playful. He's always smiling and never seems sad. He loves playing chase, and we play with balls with him. He goes to nursery and he's really popular there – he's got lots of friends.

We help Faris by playing with him and doing sign language. He has to get **suctioned** out to clean his tubes – we can both do that for him, but Dad has to do the hard things. Dad and the nurse have to do the tracheostomy tube because if it's out for too long he won't be able to breathe.

It can be hard for us, like sometimes when we want to play we have to play things with Faris instead. Sometimes we leave him out – not on purpose, but just because we want to do something for a while and he can't do everything. We can't go to a lot of places, like the cinema, with Faris because of his tubes. When we go out, we have to carry everything with us. Daddy carries Faris, so we carry the **suction machine** and everything.

Do you feel you must always play with your brother or sister?

Does a parent ask you to include your brother or sister in all your games with friends? Do you feel sorry that your brother or sister doesn't have his or her own friends? This often happens in families where someone has a disability. It also happens in families without disability – like when a brother or sister is a toddler. If you would like to have time on your own or with your friends, these suggestions may help:

- Tell a parent that you need to have time by yourself or just with your own friends.
- When your friends come to your house, ask a parent if he or she will look after your brother or sister for some of the time.
- If your brother or sister is upset or jealous, explain that you will play later when you've had time with your friends.

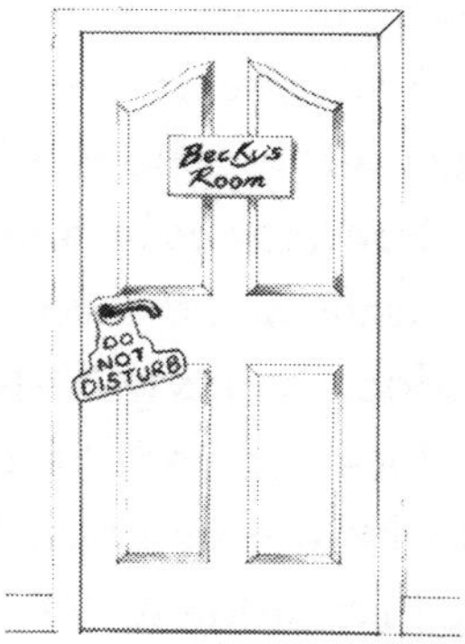

Keywords explained

- **Prematurely** – when babies are born before they are fully grown.
- **Tracheostomy** – a hole through a person's windpipe to help them breathe.
- **Gastrostomy** – a hole through a person's stomach, with a tube going into it, so that special food can go straight from the tube into the stomach.
- **Sign language** – using your hands to talk to someone.
- **Suction machine/suctioned** – a special machine to help clear out thick spit from someone's lungs.

I have to control my temper

Brandon, 10, talks about his brother Ryan, 13, who has **ADHD**.

Ryan's got ADHD. He's not been in trouble with my mam since she found out last year that he's got ADHD. He used to get in a lot of trouble before. Ever since my mam's found out, she's been crying.

It's not a real problem now, he's learnt how to handle it. Dane, my brother, sometimes says, 'Why's he doing it?' Ryan's hit him all these years. Dane doesn't understand, but he ought to – he's older than me.

Mam explained it to me; she knows I'll understand. It's not Ryan's fault. All these years we didn't find out. If he's playing with my toys, I have to play with him, play by his rules, otherwise I'll get hit by him.

The tablets what he's on, he's so much better, he hardly hits out now. Only time is when we're playing 'trippey-ups' in the garden.

Sometimes he annoys me a lot and I have to control my temper – I have to walk out the room and come back when I've calmed down. All of a sudden he'll say, 'Why did you go off?' and I'll say, 'Cos you hit me'.

Until he had the tablets he didn't know right from wrong. He looked like he was listening but he wasn't. Before the tablets he couldn't listen – he just thought, 'What's the point?' He didn't understand why he should listen.

I think if your brother is hitting you and they've got ADHD, you should walk away or stop them, play by their rules.

Do you ever get angry with your brother or sister?

Feeling angry with your brother or sister is normal. This happens in all families. Ask your friends about this and they'll say they get mad at their brothers and sisters too sometimes. That's just part of growing up together.

Some brothers and sisters have difficult behaviour and have a tantrum when you get angry with them. This is really unpleasant and sometimes can be dangerous. It is best not to yell or hit when you are angry. If you get angry a lot, here are some things that can help you calm down:

- Count slowly up to 10.
- Walk away and come back when you are feeling calm.
- Count backwards from 20 to 1.
- Go in another room and listen to some gentle music.
- Spend some time doing something relaxing – reading, drawing, making things, going for a walk outside, walking the dog.
- Tell your parents that you feel angry and need help to get calm.
- Go and play with something else for a while.
- Write a story about how you feel.
- Draw a picture about how you feel.

Keywords explained

- **ADHD** – take a look at the *Find out more* section on page 86.

Sometimes we play football on our knees

Jordi, 10, talks about his brother Daniel, 7, who has **PDH complex deficiency**.

My brother started getting what he calls a cold leg and sore neck when he was 4 years old. If he runs about a lot his foot goes stiff, his arm twists round and his neck bends over so he looks like the Hunchback of Notre Dame.

It annoys me because I can't always play a lot of football with him or sometimes we can't go out or to the beach if he can't walk. He's too big for the child seat on mummy's bike now so we can't go out together on bikes. At least with a sticker now it's easier to park the car near where we're going.

I get cross when other children laugh at him because he can't run properly. I tell them he's got problems and say if they had the same problem, would they like me to laugh at them?

I think it is bad because I can't play with him a lot as he has to rest when his leg won't move. So I try to make him laugh to stop him feeling sad. I try doing magic and do funny faces and silly walks. Sometimes we play football on our knees and using our hands instead.

Now I'm bigger I can give him piggy backs if his leg goes cold when we're out somewhere.

Can you think up some new ways to play with your brother or sister?

Siblings often learn to be creative, and think up new ways of playing, so their brother or sister can join in. This is a really great thing to be able to do. See if you can think of any new ways to do these with your brother or sister:

- Board games – let your brother or sister throw the dice every time and you move the pieces every time.
- Ball games – playing tennis sitting in chairs.

- Football – if your brother or sister can't stand up and isn't too heavy, get your parent to hold them in goal and stop the ball as you shoot.
- Word games – your brother or sister shouts out a word and you have to act it in a silly way.
- Dancing – moving fingers in time to the music.
- Pretend play – have a line of animal pictures; you pretend to be one of them, and your brother or sister has to point to which one you are.

Keywords explained

- **PDH complex deficiency** – take a look at the *Find out more* section on page 90.

I didn't see him for six weeks

Nathaniel, 11, talks about his brother Elliott, 12, who has **leukaemia**.

My mum found that Elliott was getting all these bruises and so she took him to the hospital. The hospital said it was leukaemia when he was about 7 or 8. She thought that he just kept bumping into things. It's very dangerous, it's a **life-threatening** illness. After that, all his food had to be carefully packed. It was to stop infections getting in, because they could have killed him. He had it for two or three years. He kept having blood tests; he's had 220 tests so far. He's still got to be careful; he's got to take **penicillin** for the rest of his life, twice a day.

Right at the beginning he was not so poorly, then he got worse. His hair started falling out and he refused to eat. Then he had the **bone marrow transplant**. I felt lonely and worried for him. We used to be quite close. My nan came over for three to six months because mum and dad had to go to the hospital and take care of Elliott. Mum went during the day and dad went overnight. Mum and dad never saw each other, only when they passed each other in the corridor.

A bone marrow transplant is quite risky. They found the perfect **donor**. They don't usually get a perfect donor unless they are twins, otherwise the risk is bigger. I didn't get to see him in case I gave him an infection. That made me very sad because I didn't see him for six weeks. He was let out at Christmas, a year ago. Also, I didn't see my mum. She'd promise to be back but couldn't as Elliott needed her. I didn't really speak to my nan about it much – I just wanted to forget it was happening.

It was quite strange when he came back. He still had his hair out and he looked quite ill. Ever since he's always been quite pale and I don't know if that's part of it or if it's the way he looks, because I can't remember him before. He's back to normal now. We don't talk about it because it's not the sort of thing we talk about. He still has a scar where the **Hickman line** went in. Sometimes when we playfight he complains that it starts hurting, and he stops. But that hasn't happened for a while.

I'm glad he's better. I know some people haven't recovered from it.

Do you feel fed up at times?

There are some days when siblings feel really low and fed up. Sometimes siblings think a lot about all the things that are going wrong in their life. This often seems worse at night-time when you are trying to get to sleep. At night, when you go to bed, think of 6 good things that have happened during the day. When your mind works hard to think of good things it finds it much harder to think of worries at the same time. Think of things like:

- something nice you had to eat
- something good a teacher or friend said
- something funny you saw on TV
- a good game you played
- a hug or a smile from someone who cares about you
- something you did well at school
- time you spent with a pet
- something new you have learnt
- something going well with your brother or sister.

Keywords explained

- **Leukaemia** – take a look at the *Find out more* section on page 89.
- **Life-threatening** – this means that some people can die from it.
- **Penicillin** – a medicine, called an antibiotic, to protect people from serious infection.
- **Bone marrow** – spongy stuff inside bones. It produces special blood cells (called white blood cells) that protect people against infection and make sure oxygen (the part of air we breathe) gets to every corner of the body. A **transplant** is when a person has someone else's bone marrow put into their bones.
- **Donor** – someone who gives some of their bone marrow to another person.
- **Hickman line** – a very thin tube that goes into a large vein in the chest. Then medicine can go through the tube into the person's blood.

I get fun days out too

Sian, 11, talks about her brother Dominic, 3, who has **autism**.

Dominic bites a lot. I don't know why. I think it's his way of kissing. He only usually bites when he's affectionate, not when he's angry. That's what the doctors say and I believe them. He only bites when he's having fun. It's all right. You can kind of forgive him.

When he bites you're not supposed to shout. But it's really hard not to. If you're pretty angry you've got to hold back. When you scream he thinks it's a game. He doesn't understand 'no' and he gets naughty. You have to say it calmly. If you say it seriously he understands. If you scream, he thinks it's a game and he jumps and does it again.

He's got **flash cards**. At snack time you can show a crisp or a biscuit sign. He's worked out how to use them. He's going to have a book with his signs. Then he can point to what he wants. He wants to tell you what's the matter. When he was younger and he was crying it was hard for my mum. She didn't know – does he want milk, juice or a biscuit? He couldn't tell – that was the hardest.

It's hard to explain to my friends. They ask him his name and he won't tell them. They say, 'Why isn't he talking?' and stuff like that. It's difficult to explain. I say he can't quite speak yet. I say he's got **learning difficulties** as well. Then they kind of understand. They never understand if I say autism. Some people blame the **MMR**. He lost his speech. I don't want to point fingers. When he was born, there might have been something in his head and the MMR might just have triggered it off.

Now I've accepted him not speaking, I wouldn't want him any other way. If someone could wave a wand and they wanted him to speak, I'd understand them, but I'd be a bit scared, because who knows what he'd be like? He'd be different. I don't think I'd have it any other way if I really had a choice. My mum just wants him normal – what is normal? Someone who is able to speak? The whole family's got to love him the way he is.

He gets quite a lot of attention. He gets so much that I get fun days out too. Me and my mum go shopping and to the cinema about once a fortnight. It's nice. Quite a few people wouldn't get a day out. So much effort goes into looking after him that my mum says it's nice just coming out with me. It's nice being on my own. I get extra special attention. The only thing that's annoying is that I have to go to bed before him.

Do you get enough time with your parent?

Most siblings feel they don't get enough time with a parent. It is good to have special time by yourself with a parent each day.

- Ask your parent if he or she can set some time aside each day to spend a bit of special time with you. It may need to be when your brother or sister is in bed or when someone else is around to look after him or her.
- Talk with your parent about what you would like to do together.
- Think if you would like to do any of these with your parent – playing games or making things; chatting together or talking about worries; getting help with homework; making and eating a snack together; watching TV; having a hug.

Keywords explained

- **Autism** – take a look at the *Find out more* section on page 86.
- **Flash cards** – cards with pictures to help children to communicate.
- **Learning disabilities/Learning difficulties** – take a look at the *Find out more* section on page 89.
- **MMR** – babies can have an injection to protect them from diseases called measles, mumps and rubella. This injection is called the MMR.

He really changes his moods

Emma, 11, talks about her brother Ben, 7, who has **hydrocephalus** *and severe* **eczema**.

I get on better with Ben than my brother Mark does, as they're both boys. They're always screaming while I'm dead patient. Like when we play being dogs. Ben likes being a dog and crawling on the floor. He picks up something in his mouth when I say fetch. He wants to play mums and dads but sometimes I don't play because I feel a bit stupid. He thinks I'm the same age all the time.

He shouts and goes in a mood. Last night he was really great, and then I forgot to wake him this morning and he shouted. I've done nothing. He really changes his moods. He's not really patient at waiting.

He tries to help but he always gets things wrong. If dad walks at a normal rate it's too fast for him and he's screaming at dad. He's been scratching and making a mark on Mark's hand, so it was pouring with blood.

He nips people but not me and my mam. He's both good and bad, mostly bad. Mark jumps on him and they play wrestling and then Ben gets moody and Mark says he hit him.

Does your brother or sister get very moody?

Some children with special needs can be very moody. This can be hard for the other people in the family. It seems that no matter what you do your brother or sister gets in a bad mood. The things listed below may help:

- Remember that it is not your fault – that's just the way he or she is.
- If you find there is a time of day when he or she is in a better mood that's probably the best time to do things together. (Bad moods usually happen when someone is tired, hungry, frustrated or uncomfortable.)
- You will feel better if you spend some time each day with friends who are cheerful and full of energy.

Keywords explained

- **Hydrocephalus** – take a look at the *Find out more* section on page 88.
- **Eczema** – take a look at the *Find out more* section on page 88.

I see his disability as an advantage

Amar, 11, talks about his brother Trishan, 9, who is **deaf**.

My brother Trishan is a deaf child. At the moment he is 9 years old and I am 11. Ever since he was about a month old I knew he was deaf. I was always very sad, as my only brother was not normal.

At first I was embarrassed to talk about him but now I can talk very freely about him. I now see his disability as an advantage because I have learnt a new language, **sign language**. I have also obtained a lot more patience.

Fighting was an everyday thing. We fought all the time and we still do. Sometimes I look back at some of the fights and most of them are caused because one us has upset the other or because of disobedience.

Having fights wasn't always the situation. A lot of the time we are very friendly. We often work together and get each other out of trouble. We are sometimes very competitive but lately we have built a Lego model together.

My brother is an excellent child who is a very clever child, and doesn't let his disability get in his way. I am very proud of him.

What have you learnt from being a sibling?

Growing up with a brother or sister with disability or special needs can help siblings learn to be more grown up than some of their friends. This can be a good thing. Some things you have learnt will really help you when you are older – at work or when you have your own children. Which of these have you learnt from being a sibling?

- Being understanding of people who are different?
- Knowing a lot about medical things?
- Being a responsible person?
- Feeling glad to be healthy and able to do things?
- Other things. What are they?

Keywords explained

- **Deaf** – take a look at the *Find out more* section on page 87.
- **Sign language** – using your hands to talk to someone.

She went to school in Scotland

Camilla, 11, talks about her sister Julie, 13, who has a **severe learning disability** *and is adopted.*

When Julie was born in Papua New Guinea, when she was 4, she got a sickness and became **brain-damaged**. She used to get tied to a door or tree, and just left there all the time. That's when she came to us. I was 2½ when Julie came to us.

After school she always wanted to watch Postman Pat and the Teletubbies and I wanted to watch Children's TV. It became boring for me. Sometimes when she came back from school before me, my bead-making chains were all broken, and half were missing. She used to push my dolly's eyes out. She had a very good way of getting into my room, she climbed over my gate. She took every single head and legs off my Barbies.

Two years ago she went to school in Scotland. It's much easier now. When she comes back for the holidays there's still the TV problem. Mummy tries to tell her she can't watch it as she's watched it in the day. Julie's not allowed upstairs as she'll play with the taps and in my room. She does what mummy says. She's a bit better now and started to talk a bit.

It's easier now she's away. Now none of my stuff goes missing. It's really different. It's a bit better because I can watch TV after school. The bad thing is that I miss her. I miss the way she copies me. The dog misses her. He got bonus food from her. She used to go up to him with a biscuit in her mouth and give it to him.

When she grows up it might be very difficult, because she might not be able to communicate well. Like the **Rain Man**. His brother got a bit angry with him. If you get angry it's not really their fault. You have to do something they're used to once in a while. The Rain Man liked to sleep next to a window, so in the hotel he slept next to the window. He didn't like the rain so his brother didn't go out in the rain. So like in Rain Man, I'll let her watch Postman Pat sometimes after school.

Does your brother or sister go to a residential school or have respite care?

Residential school is a school where children can live as well as have lessons. They come back home for school holidays and some weekends.

Respite care is when a child who is disabled has a short break away from home – with another family or at a place with other children or in hospital. The child can have a nice time and get looked after well, and the family can have a break from the hard work of caring for someone.

Different siblings have different feelings about when their brother or sister is away. Some siblings really like this as they get to have more time with their parents. Some find it hard when their brothers or sisters come back home again, even though they love them. Other siblings really miss their brothers or sisters, and worry if they are being looked after well. The things listed below may help:

- Tell your parent how you feel about your brother or sister being away.
- Ask to visit the place where your brother or sister will stay, and to meet the people who look after him or her.
- Make plans with your parent about how you will spend your time at home.
- Remember that your parent may need some sleep and rest first, before they do something special with you.

Keywords explained

- **Severe learning disability** – take a look at **Learning disabilities/ Learning difficulties** in the *Find out more* section on page 89.
- **Brain damage** – take a look at the *Find out more* section on page 86.
- **Rain Man** – a film about a sibling and his brother who has autism.

We have to be very patient

Oliver, 12, talks about his sister Amy, 17, who is **profoundly deaf**.

My name is Oliver and I am 12 years old. I have a sister called Amy who is profoundly deaf and wears two **hearing aids**.

Amy is 17 years old. We have no other children in the family. She has been deaf since birth so I have not known things any different. She is learning **sign language** but her main way of communicating is by **lip reading**.

Unfortunately when I was little I had problems with my speech and it was very frustrating trying to get her to understand. It's better now, but if she wants to talk to me I have to stop what I am doing so that she can understand. I have a habit of tapping people to get their attention because this is how I have to let Amy know I am talking to her.

We have to be very patient because everything takes longer when we talk with Amy and things have to be repeated several times. She is always asking for explanations when she hasn't heard things.

The worst thing about her deafness is that I can't get my feelings over to her straight away and if I am upset she doesn't understand why and I am not able to explain.

I know that things have to be different because Amy is deaf and I think of myself in her situation. I know she would feel the same if it was me and be understanding.

Her deafness has shown me how to accept other people's disabilities.

Do you find it hard to communicate with your brother or sister?

Many siblings find it difficult at times to communicate with their brothers and sisters. This may be because they have a problem with their hearing or their speech or have a learning difficulty. It can make it difficult to play with their brothers and sisters or let them know what they feel. The suggestions below may help:

- Make sure your brother or sister can see your face clearly when you are talking and your hands if you are signing.
- You might need to point to things or show pictures of things or mime things, to help your brother or sister understand you.
- When you want to explain your feelings show your brother or sister the expression on your face or a picture of someone feeling the way you do.
- You may need to tell your brother or sister something a few times if he or she forgets easily.
- If you want your brother or sister to do something in a game, you may need to show him or her how you do it first.
- Make sure you allow enough time for listening and explaining.
- Ask your brother's or sister's teacher or speech and language therapist for ideas that will help you understand each other better.

Keywords explained

- **Profoundly deaf** – take a look at **Deaf** in the *Find out more* section on page 87.
- **Hearing aid** – a tiny plastic gadget that fits inside a person's ear to help them hear.
- **Sign language** – using your hands to talk to someone.
- **Lip reading** – if you watch someone's lips carefully while they are talking you can tell what they are saying by the way they move their lips.

Helen was getting all the attention

Eve, 12, talks about her sister Helen, 8, who had **holes in her heart**.

My sister was in hospital for the first year of her life. I just remember I was not allowed to see her, I was quite upset and I felt left out. I felt that Helen was getting all the attention, even though it was in a bad way, but she was getting it.

When she was older and on the children's ward, not in **intensive care**, I visited her after school. The nurses played with me and I did not feel left out so it did not feel so strange. She had to have an **oxygen tank** everywhere she went. It was quite annoying – she had a **tube** all the time, and we had to change it, and she even had to have oxygen at night. My parents always worried if she got too cold, if she got breathless or she was choking. Her lips were always blue.

When she was 7 she had to have a six-hour operation. They repaired the holes in her heart. It was quite scary, as I had not been in hospital for years. It was strange. When she came out, every time someone saw us they would always ask how Helen was. They would ask me and I would say she was fine. They would always say, 'Hi Eve, how is Helen?' She got lots and lots of presents; I got few. Mum gave me one. And she got lots of money. I got cards saying 'Thinking of you', while she got a card with a 5-pound note in. I just pretended not to mind.

I feel relieved, now that the holes have been repaired. It feels like something has gone. She has to go for six-month check-ups. It is not as serious as it used to be. She does not turn blue any more. It is not such a worry any more. We do not have to tell her to stop when she is breathless – she can just carry on running. We do not have to think of packing the car with oxygen tanks every time we go out.

It seems strange now that she does not have to go into hospital, and it is not so serious. Visiting the hospital became part of my life and now it is suddenly gone. When I went back to hospital it was like going back in time. And then when she came out I suddenly realized I might not have to do that again.

I just feel you have to keep going. You should never feel that people have forgotten about you. They know you are there. When she was having the operation, even though people seemed to have forgotten me, and no one seemed to be caring, it is not really like that. It is just there is not time for you, but you have to keep going. It will turn out alright in the end.

Do you sometimes feel jealous that your brother or sister is getting all the attention?

In some families, the child who is ill or who has special needs gets more presents, and more people making a fuss of them, than the siblings. When they are well behaved or learn new things or come out of hospital, everyone is really pleased. It can seem that people are not as interested in the things that the siblings do. It is normal to feel jealous when this happens. The suggestions below may help:

- Talk to a parent or a friend about it. Say that you understand why other people make a fuss of your brother or sister, but that you still find it hard.
- Tell your parent about the things you are doing well at in school, and at any clubs you go to. They may have missed hearing about these, as they were worried or tired.
- Ask your parent to tell relatives and friends to be fair with gifts and attention, for all the children in the family.

Keywords explained

- **Hole in the heart** – take a look at the *Find out more* section on page 88.
- **Intensive care** – a special ward in hospital for children who are very ill.
- **Oxygen tank** – a container with oxygen (the part of air we breathe).
- **Tube** – from the oxygen tank into the person's nose, so that they can get oxygen straight into their lungs.

Our budgies are good for him

Jennifer, 12, talks about her brother Stefan, 9, who has **ADHD**.

With Stefan's ADHD, if you shout or if I tell him to leave my bedroom he shouts and then if you keep telling him he hits you. He hits me, my mam and sometimes my dad. They don't shout at him 'cos it would make his temper worse, so they just tell him to stop. It doesn't always work though – he only stops sometimes.

Sometimes he does things like kicking, and he thinks he won't get told off because he's got something wrong. I don't think that's fair. It puts stress on all the family.

Sometimes if I'm on the computer doing homework, he wants to be on and I have to let him so he doesn't kick off. It's not fair, especially with homework because I might get detention if I haven't done it.

He takes up a lot more attention than me. I write stories in my bedroom to keep out of his way, but he still comes in.

He wakes up every night and goes in my mam and dad's room – they end up tired. Sometimes they take it out on me when it's not my fault and I get upset.

In the future, he might be worse or he might get better. I don't know. I think probably he'll be calm most of the time but still kick off sometimes. Stefan's got ADHD really bad though; they said at the hospital that he has got it bad. He's worse than some other people with it.

A nice thing about Stefan is sometimes he can be really lovely in the mornings and at night-times. Once when I got up and he got up about an hour after me he wouldn't stop cuddling me. He was just being really nice – he wouldn't let go.

I think our budgies are good for him as well, 'cos he just sits and looks at them and speaks to them sometimes and I think they help calm him down.

Do you know any calm activities you can do with your brother or sister?

You may have some of your own ideas or you could try some activities such as:

- listening to quiet music
- lying on grass together and watching for birds and planes in the sky
- watching a video together
- having a parent or grandparent read a story to both of you
- tiptoeing round without anyone hearing you
- drawing pictures
- colouring in a complicated pattern together.

Keywords explained

- **ADHD** – take a look at the *Find out more* section on page 86.

I get to chat to others my age

Kirsten, 13, talks about her sister Louise, 24, who has **Sanfilippo disease**.

My name is Kirsten and I am 13. I am the youngest of four sisters. Jenny is 19, Sally is 21 and Louise is 24. Louise has Sanfilippo disease, which is a rare disease. I can remember Louise being able to say odd words and always having **carers** in our home. Some tried to boss us around and weren't that nice but some were really kind and played with us as well as Louise.

Louise has become more disabled over the years and now she can't really do anything for herself, and has to have her food through a tube in her stomach now.

Lou often makes us laugh with all the things she does but I find her quite embarrassing amongst my friends when she chokes and dribbles. I find it hard telling new people about Louise though I would never pretend she doesn't exist or lie about her when people ask about my sisters. I am glad I have other sisters who are normal and have been through the same situations as me and I miss them when they are at university, because I can't talk to Louise.

I really love going out as a family and going on holiday but we can't with Lou unless she stays back with a carer which is becoming more and more difficult as Louise is getting more disabled. But my mum and dad are always home which is good if I ever need to talk, or need them for something. We often go to a special **conference** once a year, where we meet other families with similar illnesses to Louise. I find this fun because we go on outings, and I get to chat to others my age with brothers and sisters like Lou.

Despite all Louise's problems I am really glad Louise is my sister because she makes us laugh a lot because she doesn't care what people think of her and she is a really kind, gentle person. She has taught me many things like how to deal with other disabled people, not to be afraid or wary of them. I think having Louise as a sister has helped my friends as well to understand people different to themselves.

Do you have any opportunities to meet other siblings?

There are over two million siblings with a brother or sister with special needs in the UK, both children and adults. You are not the only one with a brother or sister with a disability or illness. If you have not met another sibling like you before, it can feel quite lonely, especially if you think other people don't understand what it's like. Here are some ways to get in touch with other siblings:

- Join a sibling group – find out if there is one near you by asking someone who helps your brother or sister to find out for you.
- Contact Sibs, the UK organization for siblings, to find out how you can meet other siblings. Tel: 01535 645453. Email: info@sibs.org.uk. Website: www.sibs.org.uk.
- Chat to other siblings from all over the world on Sibkids – if you can use the internet at home, log on to www.thearc.org/siblingsupport/
- Ask your parent to help you meet other siblings; he or she will probably know a lot of other families who have children with special needs.

Keywords explained

- **Sanfilippo disease** – take a look at **MPS disease** in the *Find out more* section on pages 89–90.
- **Carers** – people who help a family look after a person who is ill or disabled.
- **Conference** – a big meeting of people who are interested in the same thing.

I tried to find out more

Stephanie, 13, talks about her brother Ryan, 5, who has **Klinefelter's syndrome**.

Ryan has got Klinefelter's syndrome – that means he's got no **muscle tone** and has speech problems and he has to wear special shoes. He used to be in **mainstream school** and now he's in a **special unit**.

When he was about 2 he got referred to the hospital. I wanted him to get cured of it. I was upset about what happened to him. I didn't understand so I tried to find out more. Mum got leaflets and I looked on the internet. It was okay. I was just worried in case he fell over.

I was worried in case he got bullied when he was older. He's got to wear special shoes and children outside can be nasty. They pick on him because they notice different things about him. I feel really upset if he gets bullied and he might not be able to fight back.

I think about the future, in case anything happens and whether they may find a cure. Something else might happen and he might get another disability. I also think he's got no confidence, so he might not speak up if anything was wrong or if someone was picking on him at school.

You can always go on the internet or get information or go to the library or get leaflets off the doctor. It's helpful if you find out what it's about.

What do you want to know about your brother or sister's special needs?

Most siblings have lots of questions they want to ask about their brothers and sisters. Questions like:

- 'What caused the disability?'
- 'Can I get it?'
- 'Why does my brother/sister have difficult behaviour?'
- 'Why does my brother/sister have so many hospital visits?'
- 'Will my brother/sister die?'
- 'Will my brother/sister learn to talk?'

If you need to find out more, here are some suggestions of what you can do:

- Write down a list of questions that you would like to ask someone who really knows a lot about special needs.
- Ask a doctor or teacher or social worker, who sees your brother or sister, to help you answer these.
- Ask a parent what he or she knows.
- See if a parent can get you some books from the library or help you look for information on the internet or get you information from an organization that helps people who have the same disability as your brother or sister.

Keywords explained

- **Klinefelter's syndrome** – take a look at the *Find out more* section on page 89.
- **Muscle tone** – whether a person's muscles are strong or weak.
- **Mainstream school** – ordinary school.
- **Special unit** – a classroom for children with special needs or disabilities.

Mum and dad buy Tosh lots of toys

Rosanna, 13, talks about her brother Patrick (Tosh), 10, who has **Landau Kleffner syndrome**.

I am 13 and I live with my mum, dad, older sister and two younger brothers. My youngest brother, Patrick, has something called Landau Kleffner syndrome (LKS). We first knew he had LKS when he was 7.

LKS means that Tosh (we call Patrick 'Tosh' at home) has **epilepsy** and **deafness** and speech problems. He also needs a lot of help with his homework and I help quite a lot and enjoy it.

Tosh's condition has made me more aware and I would like to help kids with special needs when I am older. I know it can be a challenge but I think it is very rewarding too.

I feel upset because he is not as fortunate as me or my brother and sister. But I get quite annoyed because mum and dad buy Tosh lots of toys to keep him happy about all his doctors' appointments etc.

I feel mum and dad are sometimes too involved with Tosh to give us some attention. For instance they bought him a dog (we already have two dogs and one cat) to help Tosh and give him a friend. I think Monty has helped Tosh a lot, as he finds it difficult to make friends and most of his friends are either younger or older than him.

Some kids find it hard to understand Tosh's condition. He often takes a long time to say something or appears to be ignoring you, when actually it's that he hasn't understood you. Then they become impatient with Tosh and that makes me feel sad.

Do you feel that you and your brother or sister are not treated fairly?

Sometimes adults forget that children really like things to be fair – even if their brother or sister is ill or disabled. It doesn't feel fair if people bring a present for the child with special needs but not for the siblings too. It doesn't seem fair if siblings get blamed or disciplined for doing something wrong, but the children with special needs don't. The suggestions below may help:

- Explain how you feel about fairness to your parent.
- Ask him or her to be fair with presents and to talk to relatives and friends about this too.

Keywords explained

- **Landau Kleffner syndrome** – take a look at the *Find out more* section on page 89.
- **Epilepsy** – take a look at the *Find out more* section on page 88.
- **Deafness** – take a look at **Deaf** in the *Find out more* section on page 87.

I've found this very hard to deal with

Ben, 14, talks about his sister Sophie, 4, who has **Hurler disease**.

The first time I saw her was about 4pm on a Friday afternoon. At that time we didn't know anything was wrong. It was about two years later when we were living in Devon that my brother and I found out. I've found this very hard to deal with, especially when I've had a hard day. I always think if my life would be any easier if Sophie didn't have this.

My mum has just had another child. With both parents busy my own jobs around the house have got more numerous and with GCSEs it seems that my own life has got harder.

Now everyone else's problems seem trivial. Now as I have to do harder tasks I wonder what other people are doing and whether they have such a hard life.

There is only one person who I feel has these difficulties. My best friend also has problems like these. He is the only person I have told about Sophie (however, another friend who comes over a lot has realized).

I feel that I would find school easier if I wasn't **Dyslexick** (I had not a hope of spelling that correctly) so this adds another problem to my list. I would find it easier if people knew about Sophie. However, no one does, not even my teachers (except my housemistress).

I'm generally a fairly cheerful person. So no one would ever ask about anything. I would find it easier if someone offered their sympathies but no one ever does.

Have you got too much to do at home?

In most families parents expect children to help with jobs at home – like tidying up, clearing away after meals, and helping to look after younger children. Siblings may be expected to do other jobs though, like helping their brothers or sisters go to the loo, get dressed or eat their food. They may go to their brothers or sisters in the night when they cry. Some siblings feel they have so much to do that they cannot do homework or they feel tired all the time. If you are doing too many jobs at home, the suggestions below may help:

- Talk to your parent about this. Your parent may not know that you are finding it hard unless you say so.
- Tell a teacher what it is like at home and explain that sometimes it is hard to get homework done.
- Are you a carer – someone doing most of the care for their brother or sister? If so, next time you see a doctor or a social worker, ask them if there is a young carers' group near where you live. At a young carers' group you can meet and have fun with other children who do a lot of caring, and also get a break.

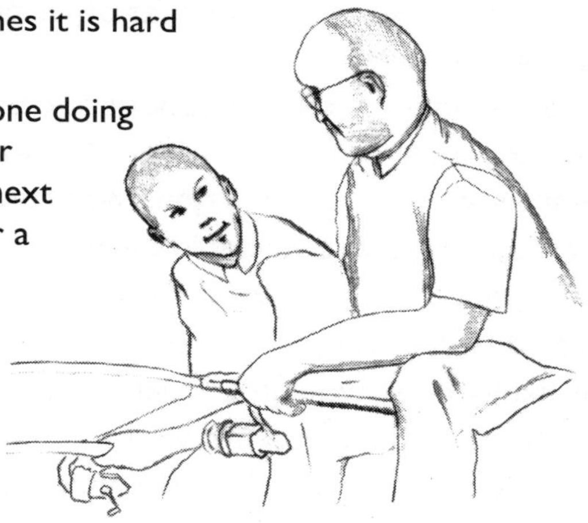

- If you really need to talk to someone and no one is available at home, you can call the ChildLine helpline for children and young people. You can call about any problem, at any time, day or night and the calls are free. Tel: 0800 1111.

Keywords explained

- **Hurler disease** – take a look at **MPS disease** in the *Find out more* section on pages 89–90.
- **Dyslexic** – take a look at the *Find out more* section on page 88.

They aggravate me

Christopher, 14, talks about his brother Daniel, 12, who has **Asperger's syndrome**.

Daniel has got Asperger's. I like the way he goes on. He does all sorts of stuff he shouldn't do. He gets annoyed, but in a funny way. Sometimes he can't understand jokes: others laugh and he can't understand. You have to say stuff very differently for him to understand. You have to make it simpler and use no complicated words. When he says, 'What does that mean?' I'll say it differently. It's automatic for me now. He can't understand. I don't suppose he's as bright as other people. It's as if you talk in another language to him.

Sometimes people at school say, 'Has your brother got something wrong with him?' He's dead quiet. He just stares at people when they walk past. I say, 'No, he's fine.' I don't want them laughing. They'd aggravate me; say he's mental and wrong in the head. I don't like that. I've not told any of my friends. They'd probably just think he was wrong in the head. They wouldn't know anything about it. I'd have to explain in detail. I could, but probably most wouldn't understand. I didn't understand at first but I've been told by doctors and my mam and special care assistants at school.

I used to always stick up for him. I started doing that from year 5 or 6. People pick on him but his head of year and my mam have told me he has to fend for himself. If someone was bullying him I would threaten them. I don't like them bullying him. He comes home crying. I think I should protect him. His head of year and my mam spoke to me because they didn't want me getting into trouble. He's got to tell the teacher instead of letting people bully him around.

I think children like him have got to learn to fend for themselves. He can't do it very well because I've been too protective.

Are you ever teased or bullied?

Siblings can be picked on sometimes because their family is different or because their brother or sister is different or because they may not feel so good about themselves. Siblings also find it hard if their brother or sister is being teased or bullied. If this is happening to you, or your brother or sister, here are some things you can do:

- Stay calm and don't show that you are upset by what the bully says.
- Ask a friend to be with you for support when the bully is around.
- Ignore the bully and then walk away.
- If you think that a group of bullies might hurt you, just give them what they ask for and then get help.
- Tell a parent or a teacher at once and ask for help to deal with the bullying or teasing.
- Call the ChildLine helpline for children and young people. You can call about any problem, at any time, day or night and the calls are free. Tel: 0800 1111.
- Ask your parent to contact the Kidscape helpline for parents. Tel: 08451 205204.
- Look at the Kidscape website. It has lots of detailed advice on how to deal with bullying and teasing. Website: www.kidscape.org.uk.

Keywords explained

- **Asperger's syndrome** – take a look at the *Find out more* section on page 86.

What's going to happen to her?

Daniel, 15, talks about his sister Ami, 11, who has **moderate learning difficulties**.

Ami's got moderate learning difficulties. She doesn't think the same as other people. I don't know what she would be like if she was normal. I've nothing to compare her with. So to me she's normal. I get on with her all right, sometimes. I play on the computer with her. I don't really know what my friends' sisters are like.

In the future, I wonder about what's going to happen to her. Is she going to get a job? I know that I can. I don't know if she would be able to. I don't know if she'll ever get one. Or if she'll ever get married and have kids. I'm worried in case it doesn't happen and I'm hoping it will.

She hasn't got many friends. She has at school; she goes along to clubs and that, but she hasn't got many friends round here. It worries me, wondering if she'll be able to go out with mates.

I can play football, go to town, go to the pictures. Even though I'm worried she won't have friends, I think she probably will. She's got a nice personality.

I worry if she'll ever get qualifications to get a job. When I was younger I didn't think about it much, because we didn't really know she had a disability until she was 9. I was 12. She's always been the same.

She's an all-round nice kid. She has her moments, mind! It's unfortunate that she was given what she's got, but then she wouldn't be Ami, would she?

Are you concerned about what will happen to your brother or sister in the future?

Almost all siblings think about this. They often don't want to talk to parents about it, as they don't want to upset them. Lots of siblings want to know things like:

- who will look after their brother or sister in the future?
- will anyone outside the family look after him or her?
- where will he or she live?
- what type of things will he or she be able to do – such as work, hobbies, getting married, having children?

It can really help if you:

- discuss your concerns about the future with a parent
- ask a social worker, or other person who helps your brother or sister, to help you and your parent talk about the future
- contact Sibs for information on helping families make plans for the future. Tel: 01535 645453. Email: info@sibs.org.uk.

Keywords explained

- **Moderate learning difficulties** – take a look at **Learning disabilities/Learning difficulties** in the *Find out more* section on page 89.

I used to love the Christmas parties

Lauren, 15, talks about her brother Matt, 17, who has **haemophilia**.

My brother Matt has haemophilia. Like everything, it has its ups and downs. When I was younger I used to think it was fun – we would visit the hospital where I got to play on all the little bikes and toys, and I made friends with the nurses. I hardly knew I was in a hospital!

I used to love the Christmas parties the Haemophilia Society would organize every year, especially when we got a visit from Santa!

As I grew older, I still enjoyed the social life we had gained through my brother's disorder. We would go to the functions where they involve the brothers and sisters of the haemophiliacs as much as themselves. There were tonnes of activities to do; it was like a mini holiday.

We then moved away and became less involved in the social side of haemophilia but living with my brother is still the same! Haemophilia has not affected his personality at all – he can still be a pain in the neck sometimes but he does not bring his haemophilia up as something to single himself out by.

Now I am older I don't need to visit the hospital with him when he needs to go – haemophilia hardly affects my life now at all. The only time I am reminded is when recently my brother has started to benefit from the disorder! He has a brand new car thanks to the benefits he receives. I know this is necessary for him to be able to drive to the hospital, but it's so unfair!

Do you get to do things that are fun?

In order to be healthy, sleep well and learn at school, children need fun and laughter. Do something each day that makes you smile.

- Read a funny story.
- Tell a joke.
- Watch a comedy film.
- See the funny side of those strange things that happen in families.
- Do something fun with your friends.
- Draw comic faces of people you know.
- Go to a fun activity with your brother or sister.

Keywords explained

- **Haemophilia** – take a look at the *Find out more* section on page 88.

Anger versus love

Emma, 15, has written a poem about being a sibling. Her brother has **tuberous sclerosis**.

Anger versus love

Anger, sorrow, love and care,
These are feelings we all share
As we have siblings – sisters and brothers,
Who are different from most others.

Frustration, crying, laughter and joy,
They're all the same – girl and boy.
But deep inside, something changed,
When the child was being made.

Worry, irritation, happiness and delight,
Don't be a fool and pick a fight.
Don't sneer or tease – being a bully,
It's stupid and reckless and not very funny.

Helplessness, jealousy, affection, concern,
It might be difficult for them to learn.
They may hang around being a pest.
But they're just people with TS.

Do you have something to share with others about being a sibling?

You have been reading about the experiences of other siblings in this book. These stories help others understand what it is like to be a sibling of someone with special needs. Write a story, poem or song, or draw a picture about what it is like being a sibling. Here are some ideas for what to include in it:

- The things you like about being a sibling.
- The things you don't like.
- The things that other people do which help you as a sibling.
- The things you wish other people would do to help you.
- How you feel about your brother or sister.

When it is finished give it to your parent. Say that you want him or her to understand what it is like for you. If you wish, you can email it to Sibs (info@sibs.org.uk) to put on their website to share with other siblings and parents.

Keywords explained

- **Tuberous sclerosis** – take a look at the *Find out more* section on page 90.

I took time out to be with him

Emma, 16, talks about her brother Patrick, 9, who has **Hurler disease**.

He's got such character – he's lively. He's won a cup at school. It's a school for blind children. He won the Diana cup for getting the most out of life. He can't see two feet in front of him. He bumps into things and then he stops. He gets up after anything. He's so bubbly, he smiles, and he's always giggling. When I look at him he's like a normal child. Though when you look underneath he has scars everywhere – his back, side, hips, head, feet, ears. It's been difficult without doubt.

All through his life he's had 12 different operations. I've been there for every one. I was the one who pushed him up and down on the ward in a wheelchair. I helped when he had a **catheter**. I've helped bandage his head after an operation. He's bounced back from every operation. He almost had to have a **shunt**. I was petrified in case I might lose him because there are chances of the shunt getting infected. He just pulled through and didn't need a shunt. It's the only one he's not pulled through quickly. We were worried. For seven or eight weeks he was in a **cast** from his hip to his ankle and couldn't move in the slightest and I helped. That was earlier this year.

I've always been to every one of his operations. He had his hip operation not long before my GCSEs and I took time out to be with him, even though it had a major impact on my results. I'm very close to my brother. I'm the oldest of four and Patrick is the youngest. I've always been there, ever since he was born. When he was little, we all had to have blood tests because he had to have a **bone marrow transplant**. We were all willing to give bone marrow and my father was the closest match. I was only young at the time and I didn't understand fully, but I would have done it. I would have failed all my GCSEs if I had to be with him. I couldn't care less about anything else.

Are you spending enough time on your education?

Your education is very important. When family life is difficult, things like school and homework can seem less important. However, when you are older you will be pleased that you made time for your school work. It will help you find a job you like and help you feel more confident out in the world. Although your brother or sister needs a lot of care, your life is important too. The suggestions below may help:

- Talk to your teacher about what is happening at home.
- Ask for help to catch up on work if you have needed to be off school.
- See if you can do your exams the following year if you have been away for a long time.

Keywords explained

- **Hurler disease** – take a look at **MPS disease** in the *Find out more* section on pages 89–90.
- **Catheter** – a tube that collects urine, or wee, from the bladder. People use it when they are stuck in bed and cannot get to the toilet or when they cannot feel that they need the toilet.
- **Shunt** – a tiny tube that is put into someone's brain, to drain away the extra fluid, when there is too much fluid around their brain.
- **Cast** – when someone breaks a bone, a cast is put on to hold it in place and help it mend.
- **Bone marrow** – spongy stuff inside bones. It produces special blood cells (called white blood cells) that protect people against infection and makes sure oxygen (the part of air we breathe) gets to every corner of the body. A **transplant** is when a person has someone else's bone marrow put into their bones.

I think, is it time for him to go?

Dan, 16, talks about his brother Michael, 12, who has **spinal muscular atrophy**.

Hi, I'm Dan and I'm nearly 17. I live at home with my mum and 12-year-old brother Michael who's in a wheelchair. He has spinal muscular atrophy, which basically means that the nerves in the base of the spine are either dead or dying which has made his muscles weak.

Michael has never been able to walk so he's been racing around in his power chair since he was 2 years old. He also has a nasal gastric tube, which is a tube up his nose and into his stomach to help him feed. Because of this kids come up and ask what it is. I often get annoyed but realize kids are just interested. I'd rather that than they stare – so what if he uses a power chair and has a tube up his nose? A few have learnt their lesson for staring. I've seen them trip up or walk into a lamp post – serves them right – it's rude to stare.

Like, everything I've done – football, cricket, hockey, fishing, rugby and lots of other things I've tried – he's joined in. Just because he's in a wheelchair doesn't stop him taking part – with fishing he had a rod that we adapted for him and went places that were accessible. When we play cricket in the garden or park, he plays with a lightweight bat and sponge ball and has his own technique of bowling with a tennis ball.

Michael in every other way is just like any brother – annoying and wants to be in on everything I do. When I was younger I did wish for him to walk and still do but I realize things now won't change but still Michael is Michael.

We've had lots of stays in hospital with bad chest infections and **IVs**. When I was younger I did think he was just poorly a bit more than other kids but now I'm older I realize the seriousness of him being ill and not getting better as fast. Each time now I think, is it time for him to go?

Although Michael is disabled, we still have good fun and he's a very funny lad with a good sense of humour but he's not like any other brother – he's special – he's Michael.

Does your brother or sister have a short time to live?

There are a lot of things to deal with for siblings who grow up with a brother or sister who might not live as long as other people. It is normal to feel sad and worried at times. Here are some things that can help:

- Make sure that you get enough time with your brother or sister. Ask a parent to help you and your brother or sister do something special together.
- Take and keep lots of photos of you and your brother or sister together.
- Keep a diary or a scrapbook so you can collect memories of things you want to remember about your brother or sister.
- Talk to a caring adult about any feelings of guilt, anger, sadness or anxiety you may have – these are all normal feelings.

- Ask for information about your brother or sister when you need it. It is better to have the facts, rather than imagine that things are worse than they really are.
- Your life is important too – ask your parent to spend time with you. Continue to do things that you really like. You will be better company for your brother or sister if are you are enjoying things.
- Winston's Wish helps children and young people deal with the death of someone in the family – they have lots of information for young people on coping with loss. You can find their contact details on page 92.

Keywords explained

- **Spinal muscular atrophy** – take a look at the *Find out more* section on page 90.
- **IV or intravenous drip** – a tube that goes into a needle in the skin. It is a way of getting food and medicine into the body if someone cannot eat or drink.

We are unable to take holidays together

Joanne, 17, talks about her sister Ashleigh, 15, who has **autism** *and* **severe learning disabilities**.

Life with Ashleigh is becoming exceedingly difficult as each day passes. Our lives revolve around her behaviour and we have to be as patient as possible. At times her behaviour limits my life considerably – for example, I may have to drop everything to entertain her. Additionally, it is difficult for us to function as a 'normal' family as we are unable to take holidays together.

We fight occasionally, as other sisters do, but generally we get on well. I admit it is very difficult with Ashleigh and her tantrums, but disability is just another part of day-to-day life. I have lived with it for as long as I can remember and to me, she is just a normal sister. It's just really hard at times.

Is it difficult for your family to do things all together?

Sometimes siblings want to do things all together as a family – like go swimming, go cycling, eat in a café. And this may not be possible because of a brother or sister's disability. This happens in lots of families, even when no one has special needs. You may feel disappointed or feel that you are missing out on things that other families do. The suggestions below may help:

- If there is something you would really like to do as a family, talk to a parent about it. Maybe he or she can ask someone to help your brother or sister join in with that activity.
- Ask if you can do a favourite activity with a friend's family or with a relative or if you can join a club to do it.
- Maybe you could do a special activity with your parent while your brother or sister is with someone else?

Keywords explained

- **Autism** – take a look at the *Find out more* section on page 86.
- **Severe learning disabilities** – take a look at **Learning disabilities/Learning difficulties** in the *Find out more* section on page 89.

I worry about Kirsty sometimes

John, 17, and Paul, 12, talk about their sister Kirsty, 18, who has **cerebral palsy**.

John

She used to bite a lot. It was when I used to have to carry her upstairs. She didn't like being carried. Kirsty can't walk or talk – she's got cerebral palsy. Once or twice she's said, 'Mam'. Her words aren't very noticeable usually.

I probably used to play with her when I was little, but I don't now. I help my mam look after her. I get her up in the morning, get her tablets, I usually get her breakfast, I take her on and off the school bus. It's because my mam's usually looking after the other three little ones. It doesn't bother me that I look after her. I don't have to pick her up much now – I've only done it once or twice, because she's getting too heavy.

People have been saying stuff about her, calling her names. I told people in the street not to say those names. They used to say 'spacker' and they don't understand what it means, so I told them what it meant and they don't use it now.

Paul

I worry about Kirsty sometimes when she's downstairs and the three little ones are playing upstairs and they come down and you don't know if she's alright. So I'll come down and check. You've got to get the others out the room.

John

My brother Terry just climbs over Kirsty. If I hear Terry coming down, I come down really fast and check on Kirsty. I run after Terry and Kirsty all the time. I look after both of them at the same time. I want to know where they both are. I worry about Kirsty when she's ill. She's had a couple of broken legs. Sometimes she doesn't eat. Sometimes she doesn't eat at all for days. If you try and feed her, she spits it back out. I worry about her when she's like that.

Do you worry about your brother or sister?

Siblings often don't tell their parents about things that are bothering them – things at school, things at home or things to do with their brother or sister. They feel that their parents have enough to deal with already. But the funny thing is that parents get worried when siblings don't talk about what's bothering them! So everyone keeps worrying and nobody talks about it. Next time you are worried the suggestions below may help.

- Talk to your parent about it. They will feel much better that you have been able to tell them about your concerns. And you will feel better for sharing your worries.
- If you really need to talk to someone and no one is available at home, you can call the ChildLine helpline for children and young people. You can call about any problem, at any time, day or night and the calls are free. Tel: 0800 1111.

Keywords explained

- **Cerebral palsy** – take a look at the *Find out more* section on page 87.

I am always offered one of his sweets

Laura, 18, talks about her brother James, 14, who has **Prader-Willi syndrome**.

James was born on 18 September 1989 and was diagnosed with Prader-Willi syndrome shortly afterwards. Prader-Willi syndrome is a rare condition, which involves an obsession with food.

My brother James is a very loving and talkative young man, who has a fantastic sense of humour. However, James requires a great deal of attention and, as a sibling, it is easy to feel left out at times.

Sometimes it is difficult to look upon your own sibling relationship. This is sometimes misunderstood by parents, who feel that silly fights are due to lack of understanding of the condition. This is often the case in my house!

James has certainly developed a greater awareness of others in the last few years, which has improved our relationship. I am the only member of our family who is always offered one of his sweets, which does make me feel special. So, in his own unique way, he gives me an opportunity to understand him.

What is special about your relationship with your brother or sister?

When you grow up with someone with special needs, there are both good things and difficult things about it. It's like this in all families, even those where nobody has special needs. Sometimes siblings like being with their brother or sister and enjoy each other's company. At other times they really don't want to do anything with them. This is normal. It is normal to sometimes feel caring and protective, and sometimes to feel totally fed up and annoyed with your brother or sister. It can feel good to think of the nice things. Make a list of these, such as:

- the things you like about your relationship with your brother or sister
- the special memories you have of doing things together
- the things your brother or sister does for you, to help you feel special.

Keywords explained

- **Prader-Willi syndrome** – take a look at the *Find out more* section on page 90.

Find out more

ADHD (Attention deficit hyperactivity disorder)
People with ADHD are overactive and have difficulty concentrating, do things without thinking first, and find it very hard to wait for their turn. Many people have problems like this some of the time, but people with ADHD have these problems nearly all the time.

Arthrogryposis
Arthrogryposis means that when a baby was growing, two or more joints in the body did not form properly. This means some joints between the bones are fixed in a bent or straightened position.

Asperger's syndrome
People with Asperger's syndrome may have problems understanding others or knowing what to say to them. They can find it hard to know what to do when they are with people. They may not understand simple jokes or know how to use their imagination for things like pretend play.

Autism
When someone has autism, their brain works in a different way to other people's brains. People with autism can have difficulty with talking and understanding what others say; they find it hard to get on well with others; they think and do things in a rigid (fixed) way, like repeating the same actions over and over again; and they don't like change.

Brain damage
The brain sends messages to all parts of the body, telling it what to do. If the brain gets damaged, either when a child is born or in an accident, then these messages do not get through, or get through very slowly. Brain damage can affect movement, seeing, hearing, concentrating and learning, or all of these.

Cerebral palsy

Cerebral palsy affects a person's ability to move and how they sit or stand. Cerebral palsy is caused by damage to a baby's growing brain, either before or during birth or in early childhood. Some people with cerebral palsy can also have difficulty with seeing, hearing, talking or learning and they may also have **epilepsy** (see page 88).

Chromosome disorder

Bodies are made up of millions of tiny cells and each of these has chromosomes inside (these are the parts of a cell that give us our hair or eye colour). Most cells have 46 chromosomes, divided into 23 pairs. If there is anything wrong with a person's chromosomes, this can cause disability or serious illness in that person. We call this a chromosomal disorder.

Cystic fibrosis

Cystic fibrosis is a disease some people are born with. It makes parts of the body, like the lungs and digestive system, produce a very sticky mucus (spit) that can clog them up. This can make it very difficult to breathe and to digest food properly.

Deaf

Deaf means having difficulty with hearing. Some people can hear some things; others cannot hear any sound. 'Profoundly deaf' means very deaf. People who are profoundly deaf need to wear hearing aids. A hearing aid is a tiny plastic gadget that fits inside a person's ear to help them hear.

Down syndrome

Down syndrome is a **chromosome disorder** (see above). Our chromosomes are in 23 pairs. Children with Down syndrome have an extra 'number 21' chromosome. Children with Down syndrome may have difficultly with learning and speaking, and some have problems with their hearts.

Dyslexic
This means people who have dyslexia. People with dyslexia have difficulty when they learn reading, writing and spelling, but often find it easy to learn all sorts of other things.

Eczema
Eczema is very itchy, dry, red skin that sometimes bleeds when it's scratched. People with eczema might have just a few patches of it on their skin or they might have it over a lot of their body.

Epilepsy
Epilepsy is when the brain sends mixed-up messages to the body, which means that the body does things it was not meant to do. This is called a seizure or fit. During a seizure, a person with epilepsy might only stop and stare for a short while or behave very strangely for seconds or minutes. Or they may fall down with their body shaking a lot.

Global developmental delay
This means that a person takes longer than others to learn lots of things like walking, talking, thinking, and doing school work.

Haemophilia
Haemophilia is when the stuff that makes blood thick and hard, after a cut or bruise, is partly or completely missing. This causes a person with haemophilia to bleed for longer than others. When they have a bruise they bleed under their skin; this really hurts and can damage their joints.

Hole in the heart
A person with a hole in the middle of their heart will get out of breath a lot, and may get more infections than other people. They may not grow as much and be underweight. They usually need an operation to close the hole.

Hydrocephalus
Hydrocephalus happens when there is too much fluid around the brain. This fluid protects the brain and spinal cord (the nerves in the backbone). Too much fluid causes pressure on the brain, and that can cause bad

headaches and vomiting, and problems with movement and learning. Doctors put a tiny tube, called a shunt, into the brain, to drain away the extra fluid.

Klinefelter's syndrome

Boys with Klinefelter's syndrome may be very tall and not have much body hair. Some are more affected and may have communication or **learning difficulties** (see below).

Landau Kleffner syndrome

People with Landau Kleffner syndrome have problems with speaking and understanding language. They can also have **epilepsy** (see page 88).

Learning disabilities/Learning difficulties

People with learning disabilities or learning difficulties find it hard to learn things. They can have different amounts of difficulties, called moderate, severe and profound. 'Moderate' means a slight amount of difficulty and 'severe' means a lot of difficulty. People who need help with almost everything, such as feeding, washing and moving, are said to have profound learning difficulties.

Leukaemia

Children with leukaemia do not have enough healthy blood cells. Blood cells are produced by the bone marrow (spongy stuff inside bones). These children need to have their blood controlled by drugs and sometimes they eventually have a bone marrow transplant (that means they have someone else's bone marrow put into their bones).

Mentally disabled

This is another way of saying 'learning disabled' or '**learning difficulties**' (see above).

MPS disease

MPS is the short way of saying mucopolysaccharidosis. Children with MPS are unable to break down the sugars in their body. The sugars stay in cells in their body, and cause damage to parts of the body. Babies show few signs of the disease, but as they get older most children with MPS have problems with moving, talking, learning and growing. Sanfilippo and Hurler are both MPS diseases.

PDH complex deficiency

This is short for pyruvate dehydrogenase deficiency. This means that there is a problem with the body so that it can't produce enough energy and the person often feels tired.

Physical disabilities

This means that a person has difficulties in moving parts of their body, because parts of their brain are damaged.

Prader-Willi syndrome

For children who have Prader-Willi syndrome, the part of their brain that controls hunger and feeling full is not working properly so they want to eat all the time. Because of this they often have weight problems. They often have learning and behaviour problems too.

Spinal muscular atrophy

In spinal muscular atrophy, some of the cells in the spine are not normal. This causes some of the person's muscles to become very weak so they have difficulties with movement. Some people are more badly affected than others.

Tuberous sclerosis

In tuberous sclerosis the person usually has growths on their brain which may cause **epilepsy** (see page 88), difficulty with learning, and behaviour problems. Similarly, there can be growths on the skin, kidneys, eyes and lungs.

Where you can get help and information

In the UK

ChildLine

ChildLine is the free 24-hour helpline for children and young people. Children and young people can call their helpline about any problem, at any time, day or night.

Website: www.childline.org.uk
Tel: 0800 1111

Contact a family

Contact a Family provides information on different medical conditions in children and puts families in touch with others whose children have the same condition.

Website: www.cafamily.org.uk
Email: info@cafamily.org.uk
Tel: 0808 808 3555
Address: 209–211 City Road, London EC1V 1JN

Kidscape

Kidscape provides advice on preventing and dealing with bullying.

Website: www.kidscape.org.uk
Tel: 08451 205204 (parent helpline)
Address: 2 Grosvenor Gardens, London SW1W 0DH

Sibs

Sibs provides information and support to siblings who grow up with a brother or sister with special needs, disability or serious illness.

Website: www.sibs.org.uk
Email: info@sibs.org.uk
Tel: 01535 645453
Address: Meadowfield, Oxenhope, West Yorkshire BD22 9JD

Siblinks

Siblinks provides a network for young people aged 13–25, who have or have had a family member affected by cancer.

Website: www.siblinks.org

Winston's Wish

Winston's Wish helps bereaved children and young people rebuild their lives after a family death.

Website: www.winstonswish.org.uk
Email: info@winstonswish.org.uk
Tel: 0845 2030405 (Helpline)
Address: Clara Burgess Centre, Bayshill Rd, Cheltenham GL50 3AW

Young Carers Initiative

Young Carers Initiative has a list of all the young carer projects in the UK.

Website: www.childrenssociety.org.uk/youngcarers
Tel: +44(0) 1962 711511
Address: Unit 2, Wessex Business Park, Wessex Way, Colden Common SO21 1WP

International sibling support organizations

US Sibling Support Project

Tel: +1(206) 297 6368
Website: www.thearc.org/siblingsupport
Email: donmeyer@siblingsupport.org

SibSupport New Zealand

Tel: +64(07) 853 8491
Website: www.parent2parent.org.nz
Email: sibsupport@parent2parent.org.nz

Siblings Australia Inc.

Tel: +61(8) 8161 6737
Website: www.siblingsaustralia.org.au
Email: info@siblingsaustralia.org.au

About the authors

Annette Hames is a consultant clinical psychologist who works with families whose children have learning disabilities in Newcastle upon Tyne, UK. She works for Northgate and Prudhoe NHS Trust. Annette has worked with children with learning disabilities for over 20 years. She became particularly interested in support for the siblings of children with disabilities when working with a small group of families who had children with Down syndrome. Parents told her that they had been given no advice on how to inform siblings that they had a brother or sister with Down syndrome. Since her original investigations and research, Annette has completed a PhD, entitled 'Young children's understanding of learning disability'. Annette lives in Newcastle with her partner Ian, and their three children, Eleanor, Christopher and Susannah.

Monica McCaffrey is the director of Sibs, the UK organization for siblings. One of her brothers has Down syndrome and another brother, who had cystic fibrosis, died in childhood. Before setting up Sibs, she worked as a speech and language therapist, and as a development worker for a disability organization. Monica lives in Yorkshire with her husband Larry and their daughters Sorcha and Róisín.

Sibling support in the UK

All proceeds from the sale of this book will go to Sibs – the UK organization for siblings, registered charity no. 1094282.

Sibs is for people who grow up with a brother or sister with special needs, disability or chronic illness. There are at least 2 million such siblings in the UK, most of whom need support and information at different stages of their lives.

Sibs makes a positive difference to the lives of siblings through:

- an information line and website
- workshops and conferences on sibling issues
- fact sheets for siblings, parents and professionals
- helping service providers set up local services for young siblings
- training for professionals working with siblings
- networks of adult siblings
- raising public awareness of sibling issues.

For support or information on sibling issues contact Sibs:

Website: www.sibs.org.uk
Email: info@sibs.org.uk
Tel: 01535 645453
Address: Meadowfield, Oxenhope, West Yorkshire BD22 9JD.

Index